AI in E-Commerce

Creating Smarter and More Adaptive Shopping Platforms

By Oluchi Ike

Preface:

In recent years, the e-commerce landscape has undergone a seismic transformation, driven by the rapid adoption of artificial intelligence (AI). From personalized product recommendations to real-time inventory management and intelligent customer service, AI is redefining how businesses connect with consumers.

This book is a comprehensive guide to understanding how AI technologies are being integrated into e-commerce platforms to create smarter, more adaptive shopping experiences. Whether you are an e-commerce entrepreneur, a developer, or simply an enthusiast, this book offers insights into the strategies, tools, and techniques needed to leverage AI for success in the competitive digital marketplace.

Through 12 detailed chapters, we will explore various aspects of AI in e-commerce, including its foundational concepts, practical applications, and future trends. Each chapter builds on the previous one, providing a step-by-step journey into this transformative domain.

Let us embark on this exciting journey together as we uncover how AI is shaping the future of online shopping!

Table of Contents:

Chapter 10: Augmented Reality (AR) and AI Integration

10.1 Bridging the Gap Between Offline and Online Shopping

10.2 AI-Powered AR Applications

10.3 Building Immersive Shopping Experiences

10.4 Examples of AR-Enabled E-Commerce Platforms

Chapter 11: Ethical and Social Implications

11.1 Ethical Challenges in AI Implementation

11.2 Balancing Automation with Employment Concerns

11.3 AI Bias in E-Commerce Algorithms

11.4 Fostering Transparency and Accountability

Chapter 12: The Future of AI in E-Commerce

12.1 Emerging Trends and Technologies

12.2 Preparing for an AI-Driven E-Commerce Future

12.3 How Businesses Can Stay Ahead of the Curve

12.4 Concluding Thoughts: The Path Forward

Further Resources

References

Author's Note

Chapter 1: Introduction to AI in E-Commerce

The e-commerce industry has revolutionized how consumers interact with businesses, enabling seamless shopping experiences from anywhere in the world. As artificial intelligence (AI) takes center stage, its integration into e-commerce platforms is reshaping the industry, creating smarter, more efficient, and highly adaptive shopping environments. This chapter provides an overview of AI in e-commerce, its historical evolution, its role in modern platforms, and the numerous benefits it offers.

1.1 What is AI in the Context of E-Commerce?

Artificial Intelligence, in the simplest terms, refers to the simulation of human intelligence processes by machines, particularly computer systems. It encompasses various technologies, including machine learning (ML), natural language processing (NLP), computer vision, and predictive analytics.

In the context of e-commerce, AI is used to enhance customer experience, streamline operations, and increase profitability. AI can understand customer preferences, recommend products, detect fraud, and even predict future purchasing behavior. By learning from historical data and ongoing interactions, AI-powered systems deliver tailored experiences to users, making shopping not just a transaction but a personalized journey.

For example, when a user browses an online store, AI algorithms analyze their behavior—what items they view, the time spent on specific products, and their past purchase history. Using this data, the platform can recommend similar or complementary products, significantly increasing the likelihood of a sale. AI also drives features like virtual assistants, automated customer service, and dynamic pricing, ensuring a competitive edge in the crowded e-commerce market.

1.2 Historical Evolution of E-Commerce Platforms

The journey of e-commerce began in the 1990s, with the advent of the internet and the first online stores. In 1994, Amazon and eBay laid the groundwork for the digital marketplace. These platforms primarily relied on simple HTML-based interfaces and static catalogs that required manual updates.

By the early 2000s, advancements in web technologies allowed for more dynamic and interactive websites. Payment gateways like PayPal made transactions secure, and search algorithms enabled better product discovery. However, these systems lacked personalization; all customers experienced the same interface, regardless of their unique preferences.

The next major leap came with the rise of big data and advanced analytics in the late 2000s. Retailers started collecting and analyzing massive amounts of data to understand customer behavior and preferences. This paved the way for AI integration, as the sheer volume of data made manual analysis impractical.

Today, AI is the backbone of e-commerce innovation. Platforms like Shopify, Amazon, and Alibaba deploy sophisticated AI models to offer personalized shopping experiences, optimize supply chains, and enhance customer service. From chatbots to real-time inventory tracking, AI has made e-commerce platforms smarter, faster, and more efficient.

1.3 The Role of AI in Modern E-Commerce

AI serves as a catalyst for transformation in e-commerce, enabling platforms to be more customer-centric, agile, and scalable. Its role can be seen across various facets of the industry:

- **Personalization**: AI analyzes user data to deliver personalized recommendations, search results, and marketing messages. For instance, Netflix's recommendation engine, which suggests content based on viewing history, has inspired similar practices in e-commerce.

- **Customer Service**: AI-powered chatbots and virtual assistants provide instant support, resolving queries and assisting in purchases. These tools not only improve customer satisfaction but also reduce the need for extensive human resources.

- **Operational Efficiency**: In supply chain management, AI optimizes inventory levels, predicts demand, and ensures timely restocking of products. AI can also automate repetitive tasks like order processing and returns management.

- **Fraud Prevention**: AI enhances security by detecting unusual patterns that may indicate fraud, such as multiple failed login attempts or discrepancies in payment details.

- **Dynamic Pricing**: AI algorithms monitor market trends, competitor pricing, and demand patterns to set optimal prices in real time, maximizing revenue while maintaining competitiveness.

Through these applications, AI enables e-commerce platforms to stay ahead in an ever-evolving digital landscape, meeting customer demands with precision and efficiency.

1.4 Key Benefits of AI-Driven Shopping Platforms

The integration of AI into e-commerce platforms offers a multitude of benefits that improve both business performance and customer satisfaction.

1. **Enhanced Personalization**

   AI tailors the shopping experience to individual users. By analyzing browsing patterns, purchase history, and preferences, platforms can offer highly relevant product recommendations. Personalization not only boosts sales but also fosters customer loyalty.

2. **Improved Customer Support**

   With AI-driven chatbots, customers can get instant answers to their queries at any time of day. These chatbots use NLP to understand and respond to customer needs effectively, enhancing the overall shopping experience.

3. **Increased Efficiency**

   AI automates many back-end operations, such as inventory management and order fulfillment, reducing human error and operational costs. Predictive analytics helps retailers anticipate demand, preventing overstocking or understocking.

4. **Fraud Detection and Prevention**

   AI systems can detect suspicious activities in real time, protecting both the business and its customers. For example, unusual purchasing behavior or location-based anomalies can trigger alerts, preventing fraudulent transactions.

5. **Data-Driven Decision Making**

   AI transforms raw data into actionable insights. Retailers can use AI analytics to identify trends, optimize marketing strategies, and make informed business decisions.

6. **Scalability**

   AI enables businesses to scale their operations effortlessly. Whether it's handling thousands of transactions or managing global supply chains, AI ensures smooth and efficient processes.

7. **Better Marketing Campaigns**

   AI-driven tools optimize marketing efforts by targeting the right audience with the right message. Email campaigns, social media ads, and product recommendations are all enhanced through AI insights.

8. **Future-Proofing Businesses**

   As customer expectations evolve, AI ensures that e-commerce platforms can adapt quickly. This future-proofing capability makes AI not just a tool but a necessity for long-term success.

AI has become an indispensable part of the e-commerce ecosystem. By delivering personalized experiences, improving operational efficiency, and fostering innovation, AI is shaping the future of online shopping. The subsequent chapters will delve deeper into specific AI applications and their transformative impact on the e-commerce industry.

Chapter 2: Personalization and Recommendation Engines

In the competitive landscape of e-commerce, personalization is no longer a luxury—it is a necessity. Modern consumers expect tailored experiences that cater to their unique preferences and behaviors. At the heart of this personalization lie recommendation engines, powered by artificial intelligence (AI). These systems analyze vast amounts of data to deliver relevant product suggestions, improving user satisfaction and driving sales.

This chapter explores the fundamentals of personalization in e-commerce, detailing how AI understands user preferences, the mechanisms behind collaborative filtering and content-based recommendations, and real-world examples of successful implementations by Amazon and Netflix.

2.1 Understanding User Preferences through AI

Understanding user preferences is the foundation of any successful recommendation engine. AI leverages various techniques to capture and analyze customer behavior, creating detailed profiles that inform personalized interactions.

- **Data Collection**: AI gathers data from multiple sources, such as browsing history, purchase patterns, clicks, search queries, and even time spent on particular products. Every interaction a user has with a platform contributes to their unique profile.

- **Behavioral Analysis**: By analyzing patterns in the collected data, AI identifies preferences, such as favorite product categories, preferred price ranges, and frequently viewed brands.

- **Predictive Modeling**: AI uses machine learning algorithms to predict future preferences and recommend products the user is likely to purchase. For instance, if a customer buys running shoes, the system might suggest workout apparel or fitness accessories.

By continuously learning from user behavior, AI ensures recommendations stay relevant and dynamic. This personalized approach increases engagement and fosters brand loyalty.

2.2 Collaborative Filtering Techniques

Collaborative filtering is one of the most widely used methods in recommendation engines. It relies on the principle that users with similar preferences will likely enjoy similar products. This technique can be divided into two main categories:

- **User-Based Collaborative Filtering**:

  This method focuses on finding similarities between users. For instance, if User A and User B have purchased several overlapping items, the system infers that User B might like a product User A has purchased but User B has not yet seen.

Example: On a music streaming platform, if two users share similar playlists, the system might recommend songs from User A's list to User B and vice versa.

- **Item-Based Collaborative Filtering**:

  Instead of analyzing user relationships, this method identifies relationships between items. If multiple users who purchased Product X also purchased Product Y, the system recommends Product Y to other users who buy Product X.

Example: In an e-commerce store, customers who buy a smartphone are often recommended phone cases, screen protectors, and headphones.

Collaborative filtering excels at discovering patterns in user interactions, but it requires a large dataset to function effectively. Additionally, it can suffer from the "cold start problem," where recommendations are limited for new users or products with insufficient data.

2.3 Content-Based Recommendations

Unlike collaborative filtering, content-based recommendation systems focus on the attributes of products rather than user interactions. These systems analyze the features of items and match them with a user's preferences, as determined by their past behavior.

- **Feature Extraction**: The system identifies key characteristics of products, such as genre, color, size, material, or style. For example, in a bookstore, features might include author, genre, and publication year.

- **User Profiles**: AI creates a profile for each user based on their previous interactions. If a customer frequently purchases mystery novels, the system prioritizes items with similar attributes.

- **Similarity Matching**: Using algorithms like cosine similarity or Euclidean distance, the system calculates how closely a new product matches the user's profile.

Content-based recommendations are particularly effective when product attributes are well-defined and structured. However, this approach can lead to a "filter bubble," where users are only exposed to items similar to their past choices, potentially stifling exploration.

2.4 Case Studies: Amazon and Netflix

Two of the most prominent examples of effective recommendation engines are Amazon and Netflix. These companies have set the standard for personalization in e-commerce and entertainment, demonstrating the transformative power of AI-driven recommendations.

Amazon

Amazon's recommendation engine accounts for a significant portion of its sales. The platform uses a hybrid approach, combining collaborative filtering, content-based methods, and real-time analytics to deliver personalized suggestions.

- **"Customers Who Bought This Also Bought"**: This is an example of item-based collaborative filtering. By analyzing purchase data, Amazon identifies relationships between products and recommends complementary items.

- **Personalized Homepages**: Each user's homepage is customized based on their browsing history, wishlist items, and previous purchases.

- **Real-Time Updates**: Amazon's algorithms update recommendations in real time, adapting to users' actions during their browsing sessions.

Amazon's ability to deliver precise, timely recommendations not only increases sales but also enhances customer retention.

Netflix

Netflix revolutionized the entertainment industry with its recommendation engine, which has become a cornerstone of its success. The platform's AI analyzes viewing habits, ratings, and user interactions to curate personalized content.

- **"Because You Watched..."**: Netflix employs collaborative filtering to suggest shows and movies based on what similar users have watched.

- **Thumbnail Personalization**: The platform dynamically changes the thumbnail images of content to appeal to individual users, increasing the likelihood of engagement.

- **Diversity in Recommendations**: To avoid the filter bubble, Netflix occasionally introduces content outside the user's regular preferences, encouraging exploration.

By delivering highly relevant recommendations, Netflix keeps users engaged, reducing churn rates and increasing viewing hours.

Conclusion

Personalization and recommendation engines have become indispensable tools for e-commerce and entertainment platforms. By understanding user preferences through AI, employing collaborative filtering and content-based techniques, and learning from industry leaders like Amazon and Netflix, businesses can create engaging, adaptive experiences that drive growth.

As the e-commerce landscape evolves, the role of recommendation engines will continue to expand, leveraging advancements in AI to anticipate and exceed customer expectations. In the next chapter, we will explore how AI-powered chatbots and virtual assistants are transforming customer service in e-commerce.

Chapter 3: Chatbots and Virtual Assistants

In the fast-paced world of e-commerce, customer support is a cornerstone of the shopping experience. Modern shoppers expect instant responses, accurate solutions, and seamless interactions. Enter chatbots and virtual assistants, powered by artificial intelligence (AI). These tools have transformed customer support from a reactive, labor-intensive process into a proactive, highly efficient operation.

This chapter delves into the evolution of customer support, the role of natural language processing (NLP) in enabling sophisticated interactions, the process of building conversational AI for e-commerce, and notable success stories of chatbot implementation.

3.1 The Evolution of Customer Support

Customer support in e-commerce has come a long way. In its early days, support was limited to phone and email, with long response times and often frustrating delays. As e-commerce grew, businesses sought more efficient ways to handle customer inquiries.

- **First-Generation Chatbots**: Early chatbots were rule-based systems, capable of handling only specific, predefined questions. These bots lacked flexibility and often led to poor user experiences when queries fell outside their programmed scope.

- **24/7 Availability**: The introduction of chatbots marked a turning point, providing round-the-clock support and reducing dependency on human agents. This ensured that customers could get assistance regardless of time zones or peak hours.

- **AI-Powered Chatbots**: With the advent of AI, chatbots became smarter. They could handle complex queries, learn from interactions, and even detect customer sentiment. Virtual assistants like Siri, Alexa, and Google Assistant further pushed the boundaries, integrating conversational AI into everyday life.

Today, chatbots and virtual assistants are an integral part of e-commerce, enhancing customer satisfaction while reducing operational costs.

3.2 Natural Language Processing in E-Commerce

Natural language processing (NLP) is the backbone of conversational AI. It enables chatbots and virtual assistants to understand, interpret, and respond to human language in a natural, conversational manner.

- **Language Understanding**: NLP allows chatbots to recognize intent, extract relevant information, and differentiate between different types of queries. For example, a query like "Where is my order?" signals a need for tracking information, while "Do you have this in blue?" implies a product inquiry.

- **Context Awareness**: Advanced NLP systems maintain the context of a conversation, enabling bots to provide coherent responses across multiple exchanges. This creates a seamless and human-like interaction.

- **Sentiment Analysis**: By analyzing the tone and emotion in customer messages, NLP helps chatbots adapt their responses. A frustrated customer may receive a more empathetic tone, while a happy customer might be encouraged to explore additional products.

- **Multilingual Capabilities**: NLP facilitates communication across languages, making it possible for e-commerce platforms to serve a global audience.

Incorporating NLP into chatbots enhances their ability to engage with customers effectively, addressing their needs with precision and efficiency.

3.3 Building Conversational AI for Shopping Platforms

Developing chatbots and virtual assistants for e-commerce involves multiple steps, combining technical expertise with a deep understanding of customer behavior.

- **Defining Objectives**: The first step is identifying the chatbot's purpose. Will it handle customer support, assist with sales, or provide product recommendations? Clearly defined objectives guide the development process.

- **Data Collection**: Training a chatbot requires access to historical customer interactions, such as support tickets, chat logs, and FAQs. This data helps the bot learn common queries and appropriate responses.

- **Choosing the Right Framework**: Developers can leverage AI frameworks like Google Dialogflow, IBM Watson Assistant, or Microsoft Bot Framework to create chatbots. These platforms offer pre-built NLP models and integration tools.

- **Designing Conversational Flows**: A well-designed flow ensures smooth interactions. This includes greeting customers, clarifying their queries, providing relevant responses, and offering escalation options if needed.

- **Testing and Optimization**: Before deployment, the chatbot undergoes rigorous testing to ensure accuracy and reliability. Continuous optimization is necessary as customer behavior evolves.

- **Integration with E-Commerce Systems**: The chatbot must be seamlessly integrated with the platform's inventory, order management, and payment systems to provide real-time updates and actionable solutions.

Building a successful conversational AI requires a balance of technical innovation and user-centric design, ensuring it meets both business objectives and customer expectations.

3.4 Success Stories of Chatbot Implementation

The transformative impact of chatbots can be seen in the success stories of leading e-commerce platforms. These examples demonstrate how conversational AI enhances the shopping experience and drives business growth.

- **Sephora**:

  Sephora's chatbot on Facebook Messenger has revolutionized beauty retail. The bot offers personalized product recommendations based on user preferences, schedules in-store appointments, and provides tutorials. By integrating AI with customer engagement, Sephora has increased conversions and improved customer satisfaction.

- **H&M**:

  H&M's chatbot helps users navigate its vast inventory by asking about their style preferences and offering tailored outfit suggestions. This not only simplifies the shopping process but also strengthens the brand's relationship with customers by delivering a highly personalized experience.

- **Domino's Pizza**:

  Domino's chatbot, "Dom," allows customers to place orders using simple conversational commands. Integrated with voice recognition and NLP, Dom streamlines the ordering process, enhancing convenience for customers and boosting sales for the company.

- **Alibaba**:

  Alibaba's AI-powered chatbot, Dian Xiaomi, handles millions of customer queries daily. It uses machine learning to provide accurate responses and even assists sellers with inventory management and marketing strategies. This has been pivotal in maintaining Alibaba's dominance in the e-commerce sector.

- **eBay**:

  eBay's virtual assistant helps customers find products, track orders, and resolve issues. By analyzing user behavior and preferences, the bot delivers highly relevant recommendations, increasing engagement and loyalty.

These success stories highlight the versatility of chatbots, from enhancing customer support to driving sales and building brand loyalty.

Conclusion

Chatbots and virtual assistants are reshaping the landscape of e-commerce. By leveraging NLP and advanced conversational AI, these tools provide efficient, personalized support, creating a seamless shopping experience for customers.

The evolution of customer support, coupled with the innovative applications of NLP, has made chatbots indispensable for modern e-commerce platforms. As technology continues to advance, the role of conversational AI will only grow, setting new standards for customer engagement and satisfaction.

In the next chapter, we will explore how AI is revolutionizing inventory management and supply chain operations, ensuring businesses can meet customer demands with precision and efficiency.

Chapter 4: Inventory Management and Supply Chain Optimization

Efficient inventory management and supply chain operations are critical to the success of any e-commerce business. They ensure that products are available when customers need them while minimizing costs and waste. The advent of artificial intelligence (AI) has revolutionized these areas, offering innovative solutions that streamline operations, improve accuracy, and enhance customer satisfaction.

This chapter explores the role of predictive analytics in inventory control, AI-driven demand forecasting, the integration of robotics in warehouse operations, and the importance of real-time supply chain visibility.

4.1 Predictive Analytics for Inventory Control

Inventory control involves maintaining the right balance between supply and demand. Overstocking leads to increased storage costs and potential waste, while understocking results in missed sales opportunities and dissatisfied customers. Predictive analytics, powered by AI, addresses these challenges by analyzing historical data and predicting future inventory needs.

- **Data Integration**: AI systems aggregate data from various sources, such as sales records, market trends, and seasonal patterns. This comprehensive view helps businesses make informed decisions.

- **Demand-Supply Matching**: By identifying patterns in customer behavior and market conditions, predictive analytics enables businesses to stock the right quantities of products at the right time.

- **Reduction of Overstock and Stockouts**: Advanced algorithms forecast demand with remarkable accuracy, minimizing the risks of excess inventory or shortages. For example, an AI system might predict a surge in demand for winter clothing based on weather forecasts and past sales trends.

- **Dynamic Replenishment**: AI-powered systems automate the replenishment process, ensuring that inventory levels are adjusted dynamically based on real-time data.

Companies like Walmart and Zara have successfully implemented predictive analytics to optimize their inventory, leading to reduced costs and improved customer satisfaction.

4.2 AI in Demand Forecasting

Demand forecasting is a vital aspect of inventory management, helping businesses anticipate customer needs and plan accordingly. Traditional forecasting methods often fall short in capturing the complexities of modern markets. AI, however, offers a more sophisticated approach.

- **Machine Learning Models**: Machine learning algorithms analyze vast datasets, including sales history, market trends, and external factors like economic conditions and social media sentiment. These models continuously learn and adapt, improving the accuracy of forecasts over time.

- **Handling Variability**: AI excels in managing unpredictable demand patterns. For instance, it can predict spikes in product demand during holiday seasons or after a viral social media post.

- **Scenario Analysis**: AI enables scenario-based forecasting, allowing businesses to explore "what-if" situations. This helps in preparing for potential disruptions, such as supply chain delays or sudden changes in consumer preferences.

- **Cost Savings**: Accurate demand forecasts reduce the need for emergency restocking or heavy discounting of surplus inventory, leading to significant cost savings.

Amazon's AI-driven demand forecasting system has been a game-changer, enabling the company to maintain optimal inventory levels while offering fast delivery options like Prime.

4.3 Warehouse Automation and Robotics

Warehouses are the backbone of e-commerce operations, and AI-powered automation has transformed them into hubs of efficiency and precision. Robotics and AI work hand in hand to streamline warehouse processes, reduce human error, and increase productivity.

- **Automated Picking and Packing**: Robots equipped with AI and machine vision can identify, pick, and pack items with incredible speed and accuracy. For example, Kiva robots (used by Amazon) navigate warehouse floors, retrieve items, and deliver them to human workers for packing.

- **Inventory Tracking**: AI-driven systems monitor inventory levels in real time, ensuring accurate stock counts and reducing discrepancies. This eliminates the need for manual stocktaking, saving time and resources.

- **Dynamic Storage Optimization**: AI analyzes product demand patterns to determine the optimal placement of items within the warehouse. High-demand products are placed in easily accessible locations, while slow-moving items are stored further away.

- **Collaborative Robots**: Known as "cobots," these robots work alongside human workers, assisting with repetitive or physically demanding tasks. This enhances workplace safety and efficiency.

The integration of robotics in warehouses has allowed companies like Alibaba and JD.com to achieve unprecedented levels of operational efficiency, enabling them to handle millions of orders daily.

4.4 Real-Time Supply Chain Visibility

Supply chains are becoming increasingly complex, involving multiple stakeholders, global networks, and varying market conditions. Real-time visibility, powered by AI, is essential for managing these complexities and ensuring smooth operations.

- **Tracking and Monitoring**: AI systems use IoT devices and GPS technology to track shipments at every stage of the supply chain. This provides businesses with up-to-date information on the location and status of their products.

- **Predictive Maintenance**: AI analyzes data from logistics equipment, such as delivery trucks and warehouse machinery, to predict potential failures. This proactive approach minimizes downtime and ensures smooth operations.

- **Risk Management**: Real-time visibility enables businesses to identify and address potential risks, such as delays, weather disruptions, or supplier issues. AI-powered risk models suggest alternative routes or suppliers to mitigate these challenges.

- **Customer Transparency**: AI systems provide customers with real-time updates on their orders, enhancing trust and satisfaction. For example, a customer can track their package's journey from the warehouse to their doorstep.

- **Sustainability**: AI optimizes supply chain operations to reduce waste and carbon emissions. For instance, it suggests the most efficient transportation routes, minimizing fuel consumption.

DHL and FedEx have embraced AI-driven supply chain visibility, enabling them to provide reliable and transparent logistics solutions for their clients.

Conclusion

AI is redefining inventory management and supply chain optimization in e-commerce, enabling businesses to operate with greater efficiency, accuracy, and agility. From predictive analytics and demand forecasting to warehouse automation and real-time visibility, AI-powered solutions are transforming traditional practices and setting new standards for operational excellence.

By leveraging these technologies, e-commerce companies can not only meet customer expectations but also gain a competitive edge in an increasingly dynamic market. As we move forward, the integration of AI in these areas will continue to evolve, paving the way for smarter, more adaptive shopping platforms.

In the next chapter, we will explore how AI enhances marketing and advertising strategies, enabling businesses to reach their target audiences with precision and creativity.

Chapter 5: Pricing Strategies with AI

Pricing is a critical factor in e-commerce, influencing consumer decisions and overall business profitability. The advent of artificial intelligence (AI) has revolutionized how e-commerce platforms develop and implement pricing strategies, enabling businesses to adapt to market trends, competitors, and individual customer behaviors in real time.

This chapter delves into AI-driven pricing strategies, exploring dynamic pricing models, competitive analysis, personalized pricing techniques, and the ethical considerations that arise when leveraging AI for pricing decisions.

5.1 Dynamic Pricing Models

Dynamic pricing is the practice of adjusting prices in real-time based on various factors, including demand, supply, competitor pricing, and customer behavior. AI-powered algorithms make this process seamless, efficient, and highly accurate.

- **Real-Time Adjustments**: AI systems analyze massive datasets, such as historical sales data, customer demand patterns, and external variables like weather or market trends, to recommend optimal pricing. For example, an AI model might increase the price of a product during peak demand periods, such as holiday seasons, and lower it during off-peak times to stimulate sales.

- **Market Responsiveness**: Dynamic pricing enables businesses to respond quickly to market changes. For instance, when a competitor offers a discount on a similar product, AI can recommend a competitive price adjustment to maintain market share.

- **Segmentation-Based Pricing**: AI tailors pricing strategies for different customer segments. For instance, frequent buyers may be offered loyalty discounts, while first-time customers could see promotional pricing to encourage a purchase.

- **Industry Applications**: Dynamic pricing is widely used across industries, from ride-sharing platforms like Uber and Lyft, which adjust fares based on demand, to e-commerce giants like Amazon, which constantly tweak prices to maximize revenue.

The efficiency and flexibility of dynamic pricing provide businesses with a significant competitive edge, though it requires careful monitoring to avoid alienating customers with erratic or perceived unfair pricing.

5.2 AI-Driven Competitive Analysis

Understanding competitors' pricing strategies is vital for maintaining a competitive position in the market. AI-driven competitive analysis equips businesses with real-time insights, enabling them to fine-tune their pricing strategies effectively.

- **Price Scraping Tools**: AI-powered tools scan competitors' websites and marketplaces to gather data on pricing, discounts, and promotional offers. This information is then analyzed to identify trends and patterns.

- **Market Positioning**: Businesses use AI insights to position their products strategically, ensuring they offer competitive prices without undercutting profitability. For example, an AI system might recommend pricing a product slightly below a competitor's to attract budget-conscious customers while maintaining value perception.

- **Predictive Competitor Analysis**: AI models predict competitors' future pricing moves based on historical data and current trends, allowing businesses to anticipate changes and adapt proactively.

- **Global Scalability**: For e-commerce platforms operating internationally, AI simplifies the complexity of analyzing competitors across different regions, currencies, and market conditions.

AI-driven competitive analysis enables businesses to stay ahead in the market, offering prices that attract customers while maintaining profitability.

5.3 Personalized Pricing Techniques

AI allows e-commerce platforms to create personalized pricing strategies tailored to individual customers. By analyzing user data, AI identifies preferences, purchasing behavior, and willingness to pay, enabling businesses to offer customized prices that maximize conversions.

- **Behavioral Insights**: AI systems track customer behavior, such as browsing history, time spent on product pages, and past purchases. These insights inform personalized pricing strategies. For example, a customer who frequently purchases premium products might be offered a bundle discount to encourage larger orders.

- **Dynamic Discounts**: Personalized pricing enables businesses to offer targeted discounts. For instance, a returning customer who abandons their cart might receive a limited-time discount to complete the purchase.

- **Membership and Loyalty Programs**: AI tailors membership perks and loyalty rewards to individual customers, ensuring they feel valued and incentivized to return.

- **Real-Time Adjustments**: Personalized pricing is dynamic, adjusting in real-time based on a customer's interaction with the platform. For example, AI might recommend a discount on a product that a customer frequently views but hasn't yet purchased.

While personalized pricing can enhance customer satisfaction and drive sales, transparency is key to maintaining trust and avoiding perceptions of unfairness.

5.4 Ethical Considerations in AI Pricing

The implementation of AI-driven pricing strategies raises ethical concerns, particularly around transparency, fairness, and potential discrimination. Addressing these concerns is critical for maintaining consumer trust and regulatory compliance.

- **Transparency**: Customers may feel alienated if they perceive AI-driven pricing as opaque or manipulative. Businesses must communicate how prices are determined and ensure customers understand the value they receive.

- **Fairness**: Personalized pricing should not exploit customers based on their perceived willingness to pay. For example, charging higher prices to less price-sensitive customers may lead to backlash and reputational damage.

- **Avoiding Discrimination**: AI algorithms must be carefully designed and monitored to prevent discriminatory pricing practices based on demographic factors such as age, gender, or location.

- **Regulatory Compliance**: Businesses must adhere to legal and regulatory guidelines concerning pricing practices, ensuring that AI systems operate within ethical and legal boundaries. For instance, price-fixing or collusion facilitated by AI could lead to severe penalties.

- **Balancing Profit and Customer Trust**: While AI-driven pricing aims to maximize revenue, businesses must balance this goal with the long-term objective of building loyal and satisfied customers.

Ethical AI pricing is not only a moral imperative but also a business necessity in an era where consumer awareness and scrutiny are high.

Conclusion

AI is revolutionizing pricing strategies in e-commerce, enabling businesses to adopt dynamic pricing models, analyze competitors effectively, and offer personalized pricing that resonates with individual customers. However, with great power comes great responsibility. The ethical considerations surrounding AI-driven pricing must be addressed to ensure transparency, fairness, and trust.

As we move forward, businesses that successfully leverage AI for pricing strategies while maintaining ethical practices will be well-positioned to thrive in an increasingly competitive market. In the next chapter, we will explore how AI enhances marketing and advertising, enabling businesses to connect with their target audiences more effectively.

Chapter 6: AI in Fraud Detection and Security

Fraudulent activities pose a significant threat to e-commerce platforms, compromising financial stability and eroding customer trust. As digital transactions grow, so does the sophistication of cybercriminals employing advanced techniques to exploit vulnerabilities. Artificial intelligence (AI) has emerged as a robust solution, revolutionizing fraud detection and enhancing security in the e-commerce sector.

This chapter explores how AI recognizes fraudulent activities, the role of machine learning in fraud prevention, its application in payment security, and the critical considerations for regulatory compliance and privacy.

6.1 Recognizing Fraudulent Activities

AI excels at identifying fraudulent activities by analyzing vast amounts of data for patterns and anomalies that might escape human detection. Fraudulent behavior can take many forms in e-commerce, such as identity theft, payment fraud, account takeovers, or fake reviews.

- **Behavioral Analysis**: AI tools analyze customer behavior in real time, identifying anomalies that might indicate fraud. For example, a sudden spike in high-value transactions from an account that previously made low-value purchases might raise red flags.

- **Pattern Recognition**: Historical data allows AI to recognize recurring patterns associated with fraud, such as repeated failed login attempts, unusual login locations, or rapid cart abandonments followed by new account creation.

- **Detecting Synthetic Identities**: Fraudsters often create synthetic identities by combining fake information with real data. AI's ability to cross-reference data points and verify authenticity makes it highly effective in detecting such activities.

- **Monitoring Transactions**: AI continuously monitors transactions for irregularities, such as mismatched billing and shipping addresses or unusual purchase volumes, flagging suspicious activities for further review.

AI-powered fraud detection systems enable proactive identification and prevention of fraudulent activities, significantly reducing financial losses.

6.2 Machine Learning Models for Fraud Prevention

Machine learning (ML) forms the backbone of AI-powered fraud prevention systems, utilizing predictive analytics and self-learning algorithms to stay ahead of evolving threats.

- **Supervised Learning**: In supervised learning models, algorithms are trained on labeled datasets containing known instances of fraud. By learning these patterns, the system can identify similar activities in new transactions.

- **Unsupervised Learning**: Unsupervised learning models, such as clustering algorithms, detect outliers and anomalies in datasets without predefined labels, making them particularly useful for identifying new and unknown fraud patterns.

- **Hybrid Models**: Many fraud detection systems combine supervised and unsupervised learning to improve accuracy and coverage, capturing both known and emerging fraud techniques.

- **Real-Time Processing**: ML models operate in real time, analyzing data and providing instant feedback on the likelihood of fraud. For example, during a transaction, an ML algorithm might flag a payment for manual review if its risk score exceeds a predefined threshold.

By continuously learning and adapting, ML models remain effective even as fraud techniques evolve, providing a dynamic defense against sophisticated cybercriminals.

6.3 Enhancing Payment Security with AI

Payment security is a critical concern for e-commerce platforms, as breaches can result in financial loss and reputational damage. AI strengthens payment security by addressing vulnerabilities and enabling secure transactions.

- **Fraud Scoring**: AI assigns risk scores to transactions based on various factors, such as transaction history, geolocation, and device fingerprinting. High-risk transactions are flagged for additional verification.

- **Two-Factor Authentication (2FA)**: AI enhances 2FA by incorporating biometric authentication, such as facial recognition or fingerprint scanning, ensuring that only authorized users can access accounts.

- **Card-Not-Present (CNP) Fraud Prevention**: CNP fraud, common in e-commerce, occurs when fraudsters use stolen card information. AI detects such fraud by analyzing transaction patterns, comparing them with legitimate behavior.

- **Tokenization**: AI supports tokenization, replacing sensitive payment information with unique identifiers or tokens, reducing the risk of data breaches.

- **Encryption and Decryption**: AI ensures secure payment processing by encrypting data during transmission and decrypting it only for authorized users.

By integrating AI into payment systems, businesses can offer customers a secure and seamless shopping experience, fostering trust and loyalty.

6.4 Regulatory Compliance and Privacy Concerns

While AI enhances fraud detection and security, its use raises critical issues surrounding regulatory compliance and customer privacy. E-commerce businesses must navigate these challenges to ensure ethical and lawful AI deployment.

- **Data Privacy Regulations**: Compliance with data protection laws, such as the General Data Protection Regulation (GDPR) and the California Consumer Privacy Act (CCPA), is essential when implementing AI systems. Businesses must ensure that customer data is collected, processed, and stored transparently and securely.

- **Bias and Fairness**: AI systems must be free from biases that could lead to unfair treatment of customers. For instance, algorithms should not disproportionately flag transactions from specific geographic regions or demographics as fraudulent.

- **Explainability**: Regulatory bodies often require businesses to explain how AI models make decisions. E-commerce platforms must implement interpretable AI systems to ensure transparency and accountability.

- **Data Minimization**: Collecting only the data necessary for fraud detection reduces the risk of misuse and enhances compliance with privacy laws.

- **Ethical AI Practices**: Businesses must strike a balance between security and privacy, ensuring that AI systems protect customers without compromising their rights or eroding trust.

Navigating regulatory and privacy challenges is crucial for building a secure and ethical AI-driven fraud prevention system.

Conclusion

AI has transformed fraud detection and security in e-commerce, offering powerful tools to identify and prevent fraudulent activities, enhance payment security, and ensure compliance with regulations. By leveraging AI and machine learning, e-commerce platforms can stay ahead of cybercriminals, safeguarding their operations and customers.

However, the implementation of AI in fraud detection must be accompanied by a commitment to ethical practices, transparency, and customer privacy. In the next chapter, we will explore how AI is reshaping marketing and advertising, driving personalization and engagement in the competitive e-commerce landscape.

Chapter 7: Visual Search and Image Recognition

The rise of visual search and image recognition technologies has revolutionized e-commerce, offering customers intuitive ways to explore products and interact with shopping platforms. By enabling shoppers to use images instead of text to find items, visual search has significantly enhanced the customer experience, while image recognition has empowered e-commerce platforms to deliver more accurate and personalized results.

In this chapter, we delve into how visual search improves customer experience, the AI techniques powering image recognition, the integration of visual search into shopping platforms, and real-world applications that highlight its transformative potential.

7.1 How Visual Search Enhances Customer Experience

Traditional text-based search methods can often be cumbersome, especially when customers struggle to describe specific items. Visual search overcomes this limitation by allowing users to upload or take photos of the products they're seeking, enabling faster and more accurate results.

- **Ease of Use**: Shoppers no longer need to rely on complex keywords or guess brand names. By uploading a photo or using their camera, they can instantly find similar products, streamlining the search process.

- **Improved Discoverability**: Visual search opens up possibilities for discovering items customers might not have found through text-based queries. For instance, a user searching for a particular type of shoes might find additional complementary accessories through visual suggestions.

- **Personalized Recommendations**: AI-powered visual search can analyze uploaded images to offer recommendations based on patterns, styles, or colors, creating a tailored shopping experience.

- **Enhanced Accessibility**: For global audiences, visual search eliminates language barriers, enabling users to search and shop without requiring textual input.

The ease and accuracy of visual search have made it a valuable tool for improving customer satisfaction and engagement.

7.2 AI Techniques for Image Recognition

Image recognition, a cornerstone of visual search, uses advanced AI techniques to identify and classify objects within an image. These technologies enable platforms to interpret visual data and match it with relevant product information.

- **Convolutional Neural Networks (CNNs)**: CNNs are the backbone of image recognition systems, designed to process pixel data and identify patterns like shapes, textures, and colors. By learning these features, CNNs can classify and detect objects in images with remarkable accuracy.

- **Feature Extraction**: Image recognition systems extract distinctive features from an image, such as edges, corners, and textures, which are then used to match similar products in the database.

- **Object Detection**: This technique involves identifying and localizing objects within an image, such as detecting a shirt or bag in a photo. Advanced algorithms like YOLO (You Only Look Once) and Faster R-CNN excel at object detection tasks.

- **Semantic Segmentation**: AI models break down an image into regions corresponding to specific objects, enabling finer-grained analysis. For instance, identifying the fabric type or design pattern in a dress.

- **Deep Learning Models**: These models are continually trained on massive datasets to improve their ability to recognize diverse product categories and styles, ensuring comprehensive results for users.

The combination of these techniques ensures that visual search systems provide precise and relevant outcomes, enhancing the shopping journey.

7.3 Integration of Visual Search in Shopping Platforms

Integrating visual search into e-commerce platforms requires a seamless combination of AI algorithms, user interfaces, and backend systems.

- **User-Friendly Interfaces**: A smooth user interface is essential for encouraging customers to use visual search. Platforms integrate camera features or simple drag-and-drop options for uploading images.

- **Product Catalog Tagging**: AI tools automatically tag products in the catalog with attributes such as color, size, and style, ensuring that the visual search engine can quickly match user queries with relevant items.

- **Database Matching**: Visual search systems connect with product databases, leveraging AI to scan and compare items based on features extracted from the uploaded image.

- **Mobile Optimization**: With the increasing use of smartphones for shopping, visual search features are optimized for mobile platforms, offering instant results through camera-based searches.

- **Real-Time Recommendations**: AI-powered visual search systems provide instant suggestions, including similar items, alternatives, or complementary products, enhancing the shopping experience.

The seamless integration of visual search capabilities makes e-commerce platforms more interactive and customer-centric, driving higher engagement and conversion rates.

7.4 Real-World Applications

Several leading e-commerce companies have embraced visual search and image recognition, demonstrating the potential of these technologies to transform online shopping.

- **Pinterest**: Pinterest's Lens feature allows users to take photos of items and discover similar products or related ideas. For example, snapping a picture of a living room setup can provide furniture and decor recommendations.

- **Amazon**: Amazon's visual search tool enables users to upload images or scan barcodes to find exact or similar products on its platform, simplifying the shopping process.

- **ASOS**: ASOS's Style Match feature allows customers to upload photos of outfits or individual items, which the platform uses to find similar clothing and accessories in its inventory.

- **Target**: Target leverages visual search to allow shoppers to use photos to locate items in-store or online, combining digital and physical shopping experiences.

- **Snapchat and Shopify**: Snapchat partnered with Shopify to integrate visual search, enabling users to shop directly by scanning products using Snapchat's camera.

These real-world applications showcase the versatility of visual search and its ability to bridge the gap between physical and digital shopping experiences.

Conclusion

Visual search and image recognition are transforming the e-commerce landscape, offering customers a more intuitive and engaging way to find products. By enhancing discoverability, providing personalized recommendations, and simplifying the search process, these technologies are redefining how shoppers interact with online platforms.

As AI techniques for image recognition continue to evolve, their integration into shopping platforms will become even more seamless and impactful. The next chapter will explore AI's role in marketing and advertising, highlighting how these innovations are driving customer engagement and boosting e-commerce success.

Chapter 8: Voice Commerce and AI

The rapid evolution of artificial intelligence (AI) has opened up new dimensions in the e-commerce sector, with voice commerce emerging as a revolutionary trend. Voice commerce refers to the use of voice commands via devices such as smartphones, smart speakers, and other AI-powered tools to search, shop, and complete transactions. This chapter explores the rise of voice assistants in e-commerce, AI-driven voice search optimization, the challenges in implementing voice commerce, and its future potential in reshaping the shopping experience.

8.1 The Rise of Voice Assistants in E-Commerce

Voice assistants like Amazon's Alexa, Google Assistant, Apple's Siri, and Microsoft's Cortana have grown significantly in popularity, becoming integral to everyday life. These AI-driven tools are now deeply embedded in the e-commerce ecosystem, providing users with hands-free shopping experiences.

- **Convenience and Accessibility**: Voice commerce allows customers to shop without typing or navigating through websites. By speaking commands, they can search for products, add items to their carts, and even place orders. This hands-free approach is particularly useful for multitasking individuals.

- **Personalized Experiences**: Voice assistants leverage AI to understand user preferences, providing personalized product recommendations and tailored shopping lists. For instance, a user might ask Alexa to reorder groceries, and the assistant remembers previously purchased items to streamline the process.

- **Integration with Smart Homes**: With the rise of smart home devices, voice commerce has extended beyond traditional platforms. Customers can use smart speakers or IoT devices to purchase items, enhancing the interconnectedness of shopping ecosystems.

The widespread adoption of voice assistants is a testament to their potential in revolutionizing e-commerce, making shopping more intuitive and efficient.

8.2 AI-Driven Voice Search Optimization

AI plays a critical role in enabling effective voice commerce by driving advancements in voice search optimization. Unlike text-based searches, voice queries are conversational and context-dependent, requiring more sophisticated algorithms to deliver accurate results.

- **Natural Language Processing (NLP)**: NLP enables voice assistants to comprehend human speech, including context, tone, and intent. This capability allows users to ask detailed or ambiguous questions, such as "What are the best smartphones under $500?" and receive relevant responses.

- **Semantic Search**: AI-powered semantic search interprets the meaning behind a query, rather than focusing solely on keywords. This ensures that results align with the user's intent, improving the overall shopping experience.

- **Machine Learning Models**: Continuous learning from user interactions enables voice assistants to refine their search algorithms, becoming more accurate over time. These models adapt to different accents, languages, and speech patterns, ensuring inclusivity.

- **Product Catalog Alignment**: For effective voice search, AI integrates seamlessly with e-commerce product databases. This ensures that search queries return results aligned with inventory, availability, and customer preferences.

Optimizing for voice search not only enhances the user experience but also positions businesses to capitalize on the growing trend of voice-activated shopping.

8.3 Challenges in Implementing Voice Commerce

Despite its potential, voice commerce faces several challenges that businesses must address to ensure widespread adoption and seamless functionality.

- **Accuracy of Voice Recognition**: Variations in accents, languages, and background noise can affect the accuracy of voice recognition systems, leading to incorrect search results or incomplete orders.

- **Limited User Trust**: Many users are hesitant to rely on voice assistants for high-value purchases due to concerns about errors or accidental orders. Building trust through improved accuracy and transparency is essential.

- **Privacy Concerns**: Voice assistants often require continuous listening to function, raising privacy concerns about data collection and storage. Ensuring compliance with privacy regulations and implementing robust security measures is vital.

- **Complex Queries**: Handling complex or multi-item orders can be challenging for voice systems. For instance, users might want to purchase a combination of products or specify delivery preferences, requiring more advanced AI capabilities.

- **Language and Cultural Barriers**: Adapting voice commerce to different languages and cultural nuances is a significant challenge, requiring extensive training datasets and localized algorithms.

- **Integration Costs**: Small and medium-sized businesses may find it financially prohibitive to implement voice commerce solutions, limiting its accessibility across the industry.

Addressing these challenges requires ongoing advancements in AI, improved system design, and a focus on user-centric development.

8.4 Future Potential of Voice in Shopping

The future of voice commerce holds immense potential, driven by continuous innovations in AI and increasing consumer adoption of voice technologies.

- **Hyper-Personalization**: Future voice assistants will deliver even more personalized shopping experiences by leveraging predictive analytics and deep learning. They could recommend products based on past purchases, browsing history, and contextual factors like weather or upcoming events.

- **Multimodal Interactions**: Combining voice with visual interfaces will create multimodal shopping experiences. For instance, users could ask for a product description while viewing related images or videos on a screen.

- **Seamless Omnichannel Integration**: Voice commerce will integrate more effectively with physical stores, enabling users to check in-store availability, reserve items, or receive personalized assistance while shopping offline.

- **Voice-Activated Payments**: Enhanced payment security measures will enable voice-activated transactions, allowing users to complete purchases with verbal confirmations. Biometrics like voice recognition could authenticate payments securely.

- **Emergence of Specialized Assistants**: Industry-specific voice assistants tailored to niche markets, such as fashion, groceries, or electronics, will emerge, providing domain-specific expertise.

- **Global Accessibility**: As AI systems become more adept at handling diverse languages and accents, voice commerce will expand globally, bridging digital divides and offering inclusive shopping experiences.

The integration of AI advancements with voice technologies promises a future where shopping becomes more intuitive, efficient, and enjoyable. Businesses that invest in voice commerce today will be well-positioned to lead in this emerging landscape.

Conclusion

Voice commerce represents a paradigm shift in e-commerce, offering unparalleled convenience and personalization. Through AI-driven voice search optimization, businesses can cater to evolving customer preferences and create seamless shopping experiences. However, addressing challenges like privacy concerns, trust, and integration costs is crucial to unlocking its full potential.

As voice technologies continue to advance, their role in e-commerce will expand, transforming how we interact with shopping platforms and paving the way for a future defined by intuitive, voice-activated solutions.

Chapter 9: Customer Behavior Analytics

Understanding customer behavior is critical to the success of any e-commerce platform. By leveraging artificial intelligence (AI), businesses can delve deeply into the patterns, preferences, and motivations of their customers. AI enables a comprehensive analysis of customer journeys, helping companies predict future actions, personalize experiences, and optimize their strategies. This chapter explores the role of AI in analyzing clickstreams and purchase patterns, building predictive consumer behavior models, improving segmentation and targeting, and enhancing customer retention.

9.1 Analyzing Clickstreams and Purchase Patterns

Clickstream data refers to the trail of digital breadcrumbs left by users as they navigate an e-commerce platform. By analyzing this data, businesses gain invaluable insights into customer behavior and decision-making processes.

- **Tracking Navigation Paths**: Clickstream analysis helps identify which pages users visit, how much time they spend on each page, and the sequence of their interactions. This information reveals which products, features, or promotions attract the most attention.

- **Identifying Bottlenecks**: AI can pinpoint where users abandon the shopping journey, such as during checkout or while browsing specific product categories. This enables businesses to address pain points and optimize the user experience.

- **Purchase Patterns**: By examining transaction histories, AI identifies recurring purchase behaviors, such as frequent orders of specific products or preferences for certain price ranges. These patterns inform inventory planning and marketing strategies.

- **Real-Time Insights**: AI-powered tools can process clickstream data in real time, enabling businesses to adjust promotions or website features dynamically to capitalize on user trends.

AI-driven clickstream and purchase pattern analysis transforms raw data into actionable insights, empowering e-commerce platforms to enhance engagement and drive sales.

9.2 AI Models for Predictive Consumer Behavior

Predicting what customers will do next is a cornerstone of effective e-commerce strategies. AI models excel at forecasting consumer behavior by analyzing historical data and identifying patterns.

- **Machine Learning Algorithms**: Algorithms such as neural networks, decision trees, and support vector machines analyze vast datasets to predict customer actions. For example, AI might predict which products a customer is likely to buy based on their browsing history and past purchases.

- **Churn Prediction**: AI identifies customers at risk of disengagement by analyzing factors such as reduced activity, decreased spending, or changes in browsing habits. Businesses can then implement retention strategies to re-engage these users.

- **Demand Forecasting**: Predictive models estimate future demand for specific products, helping e-commerce platforms optimize inventory and avoid stockouts or overstocking.

- **Upselling and Cross-Selling Opportunities**: By predicting complementary products that customers may need, AI enables personalized upselling and cross-selling strategies. For instance, a customer purchasing a smartphone might receive recommendations for cases, chargers, or screen protectors.

Predictive consumer behavior models allow businesses to anticipate needs, personalize interactions, and create a seamless shopping experience.

9.3 Segmentation and Targeting Using AI

Effective segmentation and targeting are essential for reaching the right audience with the right message. AI transforms these processes by enabling granular segmentation and hyper-targeted marketing campaigns.

- **Behavioral Segmentation**: AI groups customers based on shared behaviors, such as browsing habits, purchase frequency, or preferred categories. This enables businesses to tailor their messaging to specific segments.

- **Demographic and Psychographic Segmentation**: By analyzing demographic data (age, gender, location) and psychographic traits (lifestyle, values, interests), AI creates detailed customer profiles that inform marketing strategies.

- **Dynamic Segmentation**: Unlike traditional static methods, AI-powered segmentation adapts in real time as customers' behaviors or preferences evolve. This ensures that campaigns remain relevant and impactful.

- **Hyper-Personalization**: AI delivers personalized product recommendations, email campaigns, and promotions to individual users based on their unique profiles. For example, a fitness enthusiast might receive recommendations for activewear and health supplements, while a tech-savvy customer might see offers for gadgets and software.

- **Optimized Ad Placement**: AI analyzes user data to determine the best channels and times to deliver ads, maximizing visibility and ROI.

AI-driven segmentation and targeting ensure that marketing efforts resonate with the intended audience, boosting engagement and conversion rates.

9.4 Enhancing Customer Retention with AI

Retaining customers is often more cost-effective than acquiring new ones, making customer retention a priority for e-commerce platforms. AI plays a pivotal role in fostering loyalty and ensuring long-term engagement.

- **Personalized Loyalty Programs**: AI tailors loyalty rewards to individual customers based on their preferences and shopping history. For instance, frequent buyers of eco-friendly products might receive discounts on sustainable brands.

- **Proactive Customer Support**: AI-powered chatbots and virtual assistants address customer queries and resolve issues promptly, enhancing satisfaction and reducing churn.

- **Sentiment Analysis**: By analyzing customer feedback, reviews, and social media posts, AI gauges sentiment toward products and services. Businesses can use this information to address concerns and improve offerings.

- **Retention Campaigns**: AI identifies at-risk customers and triggers retention campaigns, such as personalized emails, special offers, or re-engagement ads.

- **Predictive Maintenance**: For subscription-based models, AI predicts when customers may cancel their subscriptions and prompts businesses to take preventive action, such as offering additional benefits or discounts.

- **Customer Lifetime Value (CLV) Optimization**: AI calculates the potential lifetime value of each customer, helping businesses allocate resources effectively to maximize retention and profitability.

Enhancing customer retention through AI not only increases revenue but also strengthens brand loyalty and advocacy.

Conclusion

Customer behavior analytics powered by AI is transforming the e-commerce landscape, enabling businesses to gain a deeper understanding of their customers and create more meaningful interactions. From analyzing clickstreams and purchase patterns to predicting future behavior and improving retention, AI offers unparalleled insights and capabilities.

By leveraging these tools, e-commerce platforms can stay ahead of the competition, deliver personalized experiences, and foster long-term relationships with their customers. As AI continues to evolve, its role in customer behavior analytics will only become more integral, driving innovation and success in the e-commerce industry.

Chapter 10: Augmented Reality (AR) and AI Integration

The integration of Augmented Reality (AR) and Artificial Intelligence (AI) is revolutionizing e-commerce, offering customers an immersive and interactive shopping experience. This chapter explores how AR and AI complement each other to bridge the gap between offline and online shopping, power AR applications with AI, create engaging shopping experiences, and showcases real-world examples of AR-enabled e-commerce platforms.

10.1 Bridging the Gap Between Offline and Online Shopping

One of the biggest challenges in e-commerce is replicating the tactile and visual experiences of physical stores. AR and AI work together to minimize this gap by creating virtual environments that mimic real-world shopping scenarios.

- **Product Visualization**: AR allows customers to visualize products in their real-world environment. For instance, shoppers can see how furniture fits in their living room or how a piece of jewelry looks when worn, reducing uncertainty in online purchases.

- **AI-Powered Recommendations in AR**: AI enhances AR experiences by offering personalized product suggestions based on customer preferences and behaviors. For example, while trying on virtual clothes, AI can recommend complementary items, such as shoes or accessories.

- **Interactive Virtual Try-Ons**: AR enables customers to try on products like clothing, eyewear, or cosmetics virtually. AI refines these experiences by ensuring accurate fitting and realistic simulations, which improves customer confidence in their purchases.

- **Hybrid Retail Models**: The integration of AR and AI supports hybrid shopping experiences, such as "click-and-collect" models, where customers explore products online using AR and then pick them up at a physical store.

By combining AR and AI, e-commerce platforms offer the best of both worlds, blending the convenience of online shopping with the tangibility of in-store experiences.

10.2 AI-Powered AR Applications

AI plays a critical role in enhancing the functionality and accuracy of AR applications in e-commerce. Through machine learning and computer vision, AI enables AR to deliver seamless and intuitive interactions.

- **Object Recognition**: AI-powered AR systems can identify and interpret objects in the user's environment, allowing for more precise placement of virtual items. For instance, when visualizing furniture, AI ensures the scale and positioning match the physical room dimensions.

- **Facial Recognition**: For industries like cosmetics and fashion, AI-driven facial recognition improves the accuracy of virtual try-ons, ensuring that makeup products or glasses align perfectly with a customer's features.

- **Speech and Gesture Interaction**: AI-powered AR applications can respond to voice commands or gestures, making the shopping experience more interactive. For example, users can say "show me more options" or swipe their hand to rotate a 3D model of a product.

- **Real-Time Adaptation**: AI enhances AR by adapting experiences in real time. If a customer tries a virtual outfit, AI can analyze their preferences and suggest other styles or sizes on the spot.

- **Data-Driven Personalization**: AI uses data analytics to refine AR experiences. For instance, it might adjust the lighting in a virtual makeup application to match the customer's real-world environment for more accurate results.

AI-powered AR applications not only improve the technical capabilities of AR but also make it more engaging and personalized for users.

10.3 Building Immersive Shopping Experiences

Immersive experiences are a hallmark of successful AR and AI integration in e-commerce. These technologies allow customers to interact with products and brands in ways that were previously unimaginable.

- **Virtual Showrooms**: AR creates virtual showrooms where customers can explore a brand's entire catalog in a 3D space. AI enhances these showrooms by analyzing customer preferences and tailoring the displayed items to their tastes.

- **Interactive Product Exploration**: Customers can use AR to view products from every angle, zoom in on details, and even simulate how they function. AI enriches this by highlighting key features and suggesting complementary products.

- **Gamification**: AR and AI enable gamified shopping experiences, such as virtual treasure hunts or interactive tutorials. These elements boost engagement and encourage customers to spend more time on the platform.

- **Social Shopping Features**: AI and AR facilitate collaborative shopping experiences, where friends can join virtual shopping sessions, provide feedback on products, and share recommendations.

- **Live Feedback and Support**: AI-driven chatbots integrated with AR provide real-time support during the shopping process. For example, if a customer struggles to visualize a product, the chatbot can offer tips or troubleshooting advice.

Immersive shopping experiences not only attract customers but also foster stronger brand loyalty by making online shopping more memorable and enjoyable.

10.4 Examples of AR-Enabled E-Commerce Platforms

Several e-commerce platforms have successfully implemented AR and AI technologies, setting benchmarks for innovation in the industry.

- **IKEA Place**: The IKEA Place app uses AR to allow customers to visualize furniture in their homes. AI enhances the experience by analyzing room dimensions and suggesting products that fit well with the space and décor.

- **Sephora Virtual Artist**: Sephora's AR application enables customers to try on makeup virtually. AI ensures realistic simulations by matching shades to skin tones and recommending complementary products based on user preferences.

- **Amazon AR View**: Amazon leverages AR to let customers visualize how products like home appliances or décor items would look in their environment. AI tailors suggestions to user preferences and purchasing history.

- **Nike Fit**: Nike's AR-enabled app measures users' feet using AI-powered image recognition, ensuring an accurate fit for shoes. This reduces the likelihood of returns and enhances customer satisfaction.

- **Wayfair's AR Feature**: Wayfair's AR tool helps customers visualize furniture and décor items in their homes. AI enhances this experience by suggesting items that complement the customer's existing furniture.

These platforms showcase how AR and AI can create innovative solutions that address customer pain points and elevate the shopping experience.

Conclusion

The integration of AR and AI is transforming the e-commerce landscape by creating highly interactive and personalized shopping experiences. From bridging the gap between offline and online shopping to building immersive environments and powering innovative applications, these technologies have unlocked new possibilities for engaging with customers.

As AR and AI continue to evolve, their role in shaping the future of e-commerce will only grow. Businesses that invest in these technologies now will be well-positioned to meet the expectations of modern shoppers and gain a competitive edge in the marketplace. By focusing on innovation and customer-centric design, e-commerce platforms can harness the full potential of AR and AI to drive growth and success.

Chapter 11: Ethical and Social Implications

The integration of Artificial Intelligence (AI) into e-commerce has brought unprecedented efficiencies and customer experiences, but it also raises critical ethical and social challenges. Addressing these concerns is essential for businesses aiming to build trust and long-term sustainability. This chapter delves into the ethical challenges of implementing AI in e-commerce, the impact of automation on employment, issues related to AI bias, and strategies to foster transparency and accountability.

11.1 Ethical Challenges in AI Implementation

AI systems in e-commerce must be designed and deployed ethically to prevent unintended consequences. Some key ethical challenges include:

- **Data Privacy and Security**: AI relies on vast amounts of customer data to provide personalized services. Protecting this data from breaches and misuse is paramount. Ethical concerns arise when companies fail to obtain explicit consent or use data beyond its intended purpose.

- **Informed Consent**: Many customers are unaware of how their data is being collected and used. Ethical AI implementation requires clear communication about data usage and giving users control over their information.

- **Manipulative Practices**: AI-powered algorithms can sometimes exploit customer behavior to maximize sales. For instance, recommending unnecessary or overpriced products can lead to ethical dilemmas about prioritizing profit over consumer welfare.

- **Environmental Impact**: The computational power required for AI systems consumes significant energy, contributing to the carbon footprint. Businesses must adopt sustainable practices to minimize environmental harm.

To address these challenges, companies should adhere to ethical AI guidelines, prioritize user-centric design, and collaborate with regulatory bodies to ensure compliance.

11.2 Balancing Automation with Employment Concerns

The rise of AI in e-commerce has sparked debates about its impact on the workforce. While automation brings efficiency and cost savings, it also raises concerns about job displacement.

- **Impact on Traditional Roles**: Tasks like inventory management, customer support, and logistics are increasingly being automated, reducing the demand for human labor in these areas.

- **Upskilling and Reskilling**: To mitigate job displacement, companies must invest in training programs that enable employees to adapt to new roles created by AI, such as managing AI systems or analyzing data insights.

- **Augmentation vs. Replacement**: Businesses can adopt an augmentation approach, where AI enhances human capabilities rather than replacing them entirely. For instance, customer service representatives can use AI tools to handle routine queries, allowing them to focus on more complex issues.

- **Job Creation in Emerging Fields**: While automation may reduce jobs in some areas, it also creates opportunities in fields like AI development, data analysis, and ethical oversight. Governments and organizations must work together to ensure a balanced transition.

Balancing automation with human employment requires a strategic approach that emphasizes collaboration between technology and the workforce.

11.3 AI Bias in E-Commerce Algorithms

AI systems are only as unbiased as the data and models they are built upon. In e-commerce, algorithmic bias can lead to unfair practices and damage customer trust.

- **Bias in Recommendations**: AI algorithms trained on biased datasets may disproportionately favor certain products, brands, or customer groups, leading to inequitable treatment. For instance, smaller or minority-owned businesses might be underrepresented in recommendations.

- **Discriminatory Pricing**: Personalized pricing models can inadvertently result in discriminatory pricing based on factors like location, income, or browsing behavior.

- **Stereotyping in Marketing**: AI-driven marketing campaigns may perpetuate stereotypes by targeting ads based on narrow demographic assumptions.

- **Addressing Bias**: Businesses must take proactive steps to identify and eliminate bias in AI algorithms. This involves diversifying training data, conducting regular audits, and ensuring that AI teams include individuals from diverse backgrounds.

Ensuring fairness in AI-driven systems is critical for fostering trust and inclusivity in e-commerce platforms.

11.4 Fostering Transparency and Accountability

As AI becomes more embedded in e-commerce, transparency and accountability are essential for maintaining customer confidence and adhering to ethical standards.

- **Explainable AI**: Customers and stakeholders must understand how AI systems make decisions. Explainable AI (XAI) provides insights into the reasoning behind recommendations, pricing, or other actions, making the technology more accessible and trustworthy.

- **Regulatory Compliance**: Governments and industry bodies are introducing regulations to govern AI usage, such as GDPR for data protection and AI-specific legislation. Businesses must ensure compliance to avoid legal repercussions.

- **Ethical Frameworks**: Companies can adopt ethical AI frameworks that outline principles like fairness, transparency, and accountability. These frameworks guide decision-making and establish benchmarks for responsible AI implementation.

- **Customer Feedback Loops**: Actively seeking customer feedback on AI-driven interactions helps identify areas for improvement and builds trust. Transparent communication about how feedback influences changes enhances credibility.

- **Independent Audits**: Engaging third-party organizations to audit AI systems for bias, compliance, and ethical considerations can validate a company's commitment to responsible practices.

- **Accountability Mechanisms**: Clearly defining roles and responsibilities for AI oversight ensures accountability. For example, appointing an AI ethics officer or creating an ethics committee can provide a structured approach to addressing concerns.

Transparency and accountability are not just ethical imperatives but also strategic advantages, as they help build stronger relationships with customers and stakeholders.

Conclusion

The ethical and social implications of AI in e-commerce are as significant as the technological advancements it brings. Addressing challenges like data privacy, employment impacts, and algorithmic bias requires a balanced approach that prioritizes transparency, inclusivity, and fairness.

By fostering ethical practices and investing in sustainable solutions, businesses can leverage AI to enhance customer experiences while maintaining social responsibility. Companies that proactively address these issues will not only build trust with their customers but also position themselves as leaders in the evolving e-commerce landscape.

The next chapter will explore how AI can drive innovation in marketing and customer engagement, paving the way for even more transformative opportunities in the world of e-commerce.

Chapter 12: The Future of AI in E-Commerce

The intersection of artificial intelligence (AI) and e-commerce continues to evolve, with new trends, technologies, and opportunities shaping the industry's future. This chapter explores the emerging trends, offers strategies for businesses to prepare for the AI-driven e-commerce landscape, and concludes with insights into how companies can maintain a competitive edge.

12.1 Emerging Trends and Technologies

The future of AI in e-commerce will be driven by innovations that redefine the shopping experience and operational efficiencies. Key trends include:

- **Hyper-Personalization**: AI will leverage real-time data from various touchpoints to create hyper-personalized experiences. Advanced algorithms will predict customer preferences even before they articulate them, offering tailored product recommendations, marketing messages, and services.

- **Edge AI**: With the rise of IoT devices and edge computing, AI algorithms will process data locally, enabling faster and more secure decision-making. For example, smart devices like virtual assistants and AR glasses will use edge AI to enhance in-the-moment shopping experiences.

- **AI-Powered Autonomous Shopping**: From fully automated self-checkout systems to AI-driven smart shopping carts, the future will see more hands-free shopping technologies.

- **Sustainability and Green AI**: AI will play a pivotal role in promoting sustainability. For instance, AI systems will optimize supply chains for lower carbon footprints, and algorithms will guide customers toward eco-friendly choices.

- **Immersive Shopping with AR/VR**: The combination of AI with augmented reality (AR) and virtual reality (VR) will create immersive shopping experiences. Customers will virtually try on clothes, test furniture in their living spaces, or visualize a product in 3D before purchasing.

- **Voice and Multimodal Interfaces**: As voice commerce matures, the integration of multimodal interfaces combining voice, touch, and visual input will make shopping more interactive and intuitive.

- **AI-Driven Blockchain Applications**: Blockchain technologies paired with AI will revolutionize supply chain transparency and secure transactions, building greater trust with consumers.

These trends highlight the transformative potential of AI to push e-commerce into a future marked by innovation and enhanced customer satisfaction.

12.2 Preparing for an AI-Driven E-Commerce Future

To thrive in the AI-driven future of e-commerce, businesses must adopt proactive strategies:

- **Investing in AI Talent**: Companies must build teams of AI experts who can design, implement, and optimize intelligent systems. Training existing employees in AI applications will also be essential.

- **Upgrading Infrastructure**: Businesses need robust digital infrastructure, including scalable cloud computing solutions, to support AI's computational demands. Partnering with tech providers specializing in AI solutions can accelerate this transition.

- **Building Ethical AI Frameworks**: With growing scrutiny around AI ethics, businesses must establish frameworks that prioritize transparency, fairness, and accountability. Addressing biases in algorithms and ensuring compliance with regulations like GDPR will safeguard customer trust.

- **Adopting Agile Practices**: The dynamic nature of AI requires businesses to stay flexible. Agile development practices will enable rapid iteration and deployment of AI solutions in response to changing market needs.

- **Focusing on Customer-Centric AI**: AI strategies should center on improving customer experiences. Gathering insights from user feedback and behavior analytics will help refine AI implementations to better serve customers.

- **Collaborating with AI Innovators**: Partnering with AI startups, research institutions, and tech giants can help businesses access cutting-edge solutions and stay at the forefront of innovation.

By preparing for AI's growing influence, businesses can align themselves with emerging opportunities and future-proof their operations.

12.3 How Businesses Can Stay Ahead of the Curve

To maintain a competitive edge in an AI-driven e-commerce landscape, businesses must go beyond merely adopting AI and strive to lead in its application:

- **Continuous Learning and Innovation**: Staying ahead means constantly innovating and learning from AI-driven trends. Businesses should encourage a culture of experimentation where teams test new technologies and refine their applications.

- **Data-Driven Decision Making**: Companies should prioritize data as their most valuable asset. Investing in advanced analytics tools and ensuring data quality will help AI systems generate more accurate insights and predictions.

- **Customer Engagement**: Businesses can differentiate themselves by using AI to enhance customer engagement. Proactive customer support, personalized loyalty programs, and interactive shopping experiences will keep customers coming back.

- **Global Reach with AI Localization**: AI can help businesses tailor their offerings to different markets by understanding cultural nuances and preferences. Localization strategies powered by AI can make products and services more appealing to diverse audiences.

- **Sustainability Leadership**: Companies that leverage AI for sustainable practices will stand out in an era where consumers value environmental responsibility. Highlighting AI's role in reducing waste and promoting green initiatives can enhance brand reputation.

- **Leveraging Predictive AI**: Predictive analytics can provide businesses with foresight into market trends, customer needs, and potential disruptions. Using these insights strategically will enable businesses to act preemptively rather than reactively.

By embracing these approaches, businesses can not only adapt to AI's future but also lead its transformation in the e-commerce industry.

12.4 Concluding Thoughts: The Path Forward

The integration of AI into e-commerce represents a monumental shift in how businesses operate and how customers shop. From revolutionizing personalization and security to enabling immersive experiences and operational efficiencies, AI is reshaping the industry at every level.

However, the path forward is not without challenges. Ethical considerations, workforce impacts, and regulatory compliance will remain central to discussions about AI's role in commerce. Businesses must navigate these complexities while embracing innovation to ensure that AI enhances the e-commerce ecosystem sustainably and inclusively.

As we look to the future, the success of AI in e-commerce will depend on the collaboration between technology providers, businesses, policymakers, and consumers. By fostering trust, promoting inclusivity, and prioritizing customer-centric design, the industry can unlock the full potential of AI to create smarter, more adaptive shopping platforms that benefit everyone.

The journey into AI-powered e-commerce is just beginning, and the opportunities it presents are as vast as they are transformative. For businesses willing to embrace this evolution, the future holds limitless possibilities for growth, innovation, and customer engagement.

Further Resources

To expand your knowledge on AI in e-commerce and stay updated on the latest developments, here are some books, articles, and online resources to consider:

Books

1. **"AI Superpowers: China, Silicon Valley, and the New World Order" by Kai-Fu Lee**
   Explores how AI is shaping industries globally, including commerce, and provides valuable insights into future opportunities.

2. **"Prediction Machines: The Simple Economics of Artificial Intelligence" by Ajay Agrawal, Joshua Gans, and Avi Goldfarb**
   Offers a practical understanding of how AI impacts decision-making in businesses, with applications relevant to e-commerce.

3. **"Artificial Intelligence for Business: A Roadmap for Getting Started with AI" by Doug Rose**
   A beginner-friendly guide to integrating AI into business processes, including retail and e-commerce.

4. **"Data Science for Business: What You Need to Know about Data Mining and Data-Analytic Thinking" by Foster Provost and Tom Fawcett**
   Provides foundational knowledge for understanding data-driven AI applications in customer behavior analytics and decision-making.

Articles and Research Papers

1. **"The Future of AI in Retail and E-commerce" by McKinsey & Company**

   Discusses the strategic use of AI in retail and e-commerce to enhance customer experience and operational efficiency.

   Read here

2. **"How AI Is Transforming the E-commerce Industry" by Forbes**

   An insightful article on AI applications such as chatbots, recommendation engines, and dynamic pricing.

   Read here

3. **"The Role of Artificial Intelligence in E-Commerce Personalization" by ResearchGate**

   A comprehensive academic study detailing AI's impact on creating personalized shopping experiences.

   Visit ResearchGate

Online Courses and Certifications

1. **Coursera – "AI For Everyone" by Andrew Ng**

   A beginner-friendly course introducing the basic concepts of AI and its applications in various industries, including e-commerce.

   Enroll here

2. **edX – "Artificial Intelligence in Business"**

   A course focused on practical AI applications for business strategies, ideal for understanding e-commerce-specific use cases.

   Learn more

3. **Udemy – "Artificial Intelligence in E-Commerce"**

   A specialized course covering AI tools, strategies, and case studies relevant to the e-commerce industry.

   Find the course

Websites and Blogs

1. **OpenAI Blog**

   Stay updated on the latest advancements in AI technologies, including their potential impact on retail and e-commerce.

   Visit OpenAI Blog

2. **TechCrunch – E-commerce and AI Section**

   Covers breaking news, innovations, and analysis on AI applications in e-commerce.

   Visit TechCrunch

3. **BigCommerce Blog**

   Practical advice and insights on implementing AI and automation in online stores.

   Visit BigCommerce Blog

Tools and Platforms

1. **Google Cloud AI Solutions for Retail**

   Explore AI tools tailored for e-commerce, including visual search, product recommendations, and customer analytics.

   Explore here

2. **IBM Watson Commerce**

   A suite of AI-driven tools for personalizing customer interactions and optimizing retail operations.

   Learn more

3. **Shopify AI Features**

   Learn about AI-powered features offered by Shopify, including chatbots, analytics, and dynamic pricing.

   Visit Shopify

Conferences and Events

1. **Retail AI Summit**

   An annual event that brings together e-commerce leaders and AI innovators to discuss trends and solutions.

   Visit the official website

2. **AI in E-Commerce Expo**

   A global conference showcasing cutting-edge AI technologies tailored for the retail and e-commerce sectors.

   Find more details

3. **Web Summit – AI Track**

   Features discussions and panels on AI's transformative role in e-commerce and other industries.

   Visit Web Summit

Communities and Forums

1. **Kaggle**

   Join a community of AI practitioners and explore datasets and projects related to e-commerce analytics.

   Visit Kaggle

2. **Reddit – r/Ecommerce and r/MachineLearning**

   Participate in discussions on the latest trends and innovations in e-commerce and AI.

   Visit Reddit

3. **LinkedIn Groups**

   Join groups like "AI for Retail and E-commerce" to connect with professionals and stay updated on the latest industry developments.

These resources provide a wealth of information to deepen your understanding of AI in e-commerce and help you stay at the forefront of this transformative industry.

References

Below are references to credible books, articles, and online sources that were used or can further support the topics covered in this book:

Books

1. Agrawal, A., Gans, J., & Goldfarb, A. (2018).
   Prediction Machines: The Simple Economics of Artificial Intelligence.
   Harvard Business Review Press.

2. Lee, K.-F. (2018).
   AI Superpowers: China, Silicon Valley, and the New World Order.
   Houghton Mifflin Harcourt.

3. Rose, D. (2020).
   Artificial Intelligence for Business: A Roadmap for Getting Started with AI.
   Pearson Education.

4. Provost, F., & Fawcett, T. (2013).
   Data Science for Business: What You Need to Know about Data Mining and Data-Analytic Thinking.
   O'Reilly Media.

Articles and Research Papers

1. McKinsey & Company. (2023).
   "The Future of AI in Retail and E-commerce."
   Retrieved from https://www.mckinsey.com

2. Forbes. (2023).

   "How AI Is Transforming the E-Commerce Industry."

   Available at https://www.forbes.com

3. ResearchGate. (2023).

   "The Role of Artificial Intelligence in E-Commerce Personalization."

   Available at https://www.researchgate.net

Web Resources

1. OpenAI Blog.

   "Advancements in AI Technology."

   Retrieved from https://www.openai.com/blog

2. BigCommerce.

   "Using AI to Drive E-Commerce Innovation."

   Retrieved from https://www.bigcommerce.com/blog

3. Shopify.

   "AI-Powered E-Commerce Solutions."

   Retrieved from https://www.shopify.com

4. TechCrunch.

   "AI in Retail and E-Commerce."

   Retrieved from https://techcrunch.com

Case Studies

1. Amazon Personalization Engine.

   Information sourced from company reports and public case studies.

   Retrieved from https://www.amazon.science

2. Netflix Recommendation Algorithm.

   "The Netflix Tech Blog."

   Retrieved from https://netflixtechblog.com

Courses and Platforms

1. Coursera – "AI For Everyone" by Andrew Ng.

   Available at https://www.coursera.org

2. edX – "Artificial Intelligence in Business."

   Accessed via https://www.edx.org

3. Kaggle.

   "Datasets and Projects in E-Commerce Analytics."

   Available at https://www.kaggle.com

These references will provide further reading and validation for the topics discussed in this book. They include both foundational knowledge and cutting-edge advancements, offering readers a comprehensive understanding of AI in e-commerce.

Author's Note

Dear Reader,

Thank you for embarking on this journey through the fascinating world of artificial intelligence in e-commerce. Writing this book has been a deeply rewarding experience, fueled by a passion for exploring the transformative power of AI and its implications for the shopping platforms of today and tomorrow.

The intersection of AI and e-commerce represents one of the most exciting developments in technology, reshaping how businesses operate and how customers interact with brands. From personalized recommendations to advanced fraud detection, AI has become a cornerstone for innovation and growth in the digital retail space. My aim with this book is to demystify these concepts, provide practical insights, and inspire businesses to embrace AI-driven solutions responsibly and effectively.

This book is not just a guide to understanding how AI is shaping e-commerce; it is also a call to action. Whether you're an entrepreneur, a business leader, a technologist, or simply someone curious about the future of online shopping, I hope these chapters spark new ideas and encourage you to explore the potential of AI in your own ventures.

Throughout this book, I've drawn from a wide range of resources, case studies, and real-world examples to illustrate how AI is transforming the e-commerce landscape. While I've done my best to present the most accurate and up-to-date information, technology evolves rapidly, and what feels like cutting-edge today may soon be standard practice.

Finally, I'd like to express my gratitude to the pioneers, innovators, and researchers who have paved the way for the advancements we discuss here. Their work has not only made AI more accessible but also opened up endless possibilities for industries across the globe.

I encourage you to think critically about the ethical and social implications of AI. Technology is a powerful tool, but its true value lies in how we use it to solve problems, improve lives, and create a better future for all.

Thank you for allowing me to share this exploration with you. I hope this book becomes a valuable resource and a source of inspiration in your journey through the dynamic world of AI-powered e-commerce.

Warm regards,
Oluchi Ike